I want to be A PUPPETEER

Ivan Bulloch & Diane James

STARRING

TOM

CARLI

JASON

NICOLE

LIZZIE

JORDAN

TWO-CAN
in association with
WATTS BOOKS

Photography © Fiona Pragoff
Illustrations Debi Ani
Design Assistant Lisa Nutt

This edition published in 1996 by
Two-Can Publishing Ltd, 346 Old Street, London EC1V 9NQ
in association with
Watts Books, 96 Leonard Street, London EC2A 4RH

Printed and bound by Wing King Tong (Hong Kong)

2 4 6 8 10 9 7 5 3 1

A catalogue record for this book is available from the British Library

ISBN 1-85434-352-1 (hardback)
ISBN 1-85434-353-X (paperback)

CONTENTS

I WANT TO BE . . . 4

FINGER PUPPETS . . . 6

SOCK AND GLOVE . . . 8

TWIST AND TURN . . . 10

ARMS AND LEGS . . . 12

STAGE STRUCK! . . . 14

SHADOWS . . . 16

LIGHT UP! . . . 18

PULL A STRING . . . 20

ON ALL FOURS! . . . 22

STRING SHOW . . . 24

IT'S BIG! . . . 26

GETTING READY . . . 28

SHOWTIME . . . 30

I WANT TO BE A PUPPETEER

As a puppeteer you will certainly be busy. There are puppets to make, a stage to build, scenery and props to gather and lots of practising. You will have to get to know your puppets well. The puppeteer is the person who has to control the puppets and bring them alive! There are lots of different kinds of puppets and by the end of this book you will have met all of them!

Put on a shadow puppet show for your friends

Find out how to make all sorts of puppets, including string puppets

Finger puppets are great for an instant performance

Discover how to bring a kitchen mop alive!

The puppeteer has to turn a puppet into a character. It may be the way a puppet moves, or speaks

FINGER PUPPETS

This is a great way to start puppeteering because you can have puppets at your fingertips almost instantly!

Hair raiser!

Roll up a tube of coloured paper or tissue paper and make scissors snips in one end. Poke it into the top of your finger puppet for a good head of hair. Or make two slits opposite each other in the tube and slot a hair style in – like the one opposite!

Choose a character first and give it a face

Shredded paper makes great hair for a jolly finger puppet

Body tube

Cut a strip of paper wide enough to fit the top of your finger above the knuckle. It should be long enough to wrap around your finger and tape in place. Cut a face shape from a piece of paper or thin card. You can either draw the features on, or cut shapes from coloured paper and glue them on. When you are happy with the face, glue it to the body tube.

You guessed right! I'm Mr Happy!

Wiggle your finger to make the puppet move about!

It's amazing how much a different hair-style can change the look of a puppet!

Who am I?

When *you* are acting you can change your expression, move around and make gestures with your arms. Puppets depend on the puppeteer to bring them to life! You can make them move, make them talk, and with some puppets you can even change their expressions. Look at the sock puppets on the next page!

Try to keep the puppets facing the audience

Don't call me big nose!

SOCK AND GLOVE

Here's a challenge! How can you turn a sock and two face flannels into a couple of cheeky puppets?

Zzzzzzzz! That looks like a good flower!

Very handy

Puppets that fit on your hand are called glove puppets. Some have a head and arms which you operate with your fingers. Others, like the ones here are simpler, but they still have loads of character.

Sew loops of wool through the top of the sock for hair

Look out for cotton balls in craft shops. They are very light and make excellent eyes. Paint them and glue them on to your puppets.

Super socks

You can turn a sock into a puppet instantly without adding anything at all, but eyes and hair help to give it personality. Put your thumb in the heel and the rest of your fingers in the toe of the sock.

8

Sew what!

Put your hand on a piece of paper – fingers closed together – and draw round it. Use this shape as a pattern and cut out two pieces of fabric. We used two face flannels but you could use felt or any material that doesn't fray. Put one piece on top of the other and start sewing round the outside.

He looks like something I wash my face with!

Buttons make good eyes, too!

Hands in!

Put your whole hand inside and see what you can do to move the puppet around.

When you get near the top of the head, lay some short lengths of thick wool between the two pieces. Keep stitching and you'll trap the wool and give your puppet a head of hair! Glue on two cotton balls for eyes and a long piece of wool to make a combined mouth and nose.

That's odd, that stripy chap looks just like a sock!

To make a sad puppet, turn the mouth downwards!

TWIST AND TURN

Here is another kind of puppet that is easy to make and operate. All the puppets here are known as rod or stick puppets. The rod acts as the back for the puppet and also moves the puppet around.

Mop it up!
String or sponge mops can become puppets within seconds. They just need a clever puppeteer to bring them to life.

Add a nose and two ribbons to a string mop to make a cute dog

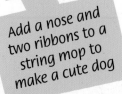

It's up to you!
Good organization and lots of practise are vital when you come to put on a show! You may well end up being the only puppeteer with a large cast of puppets to deal with!

I'm so sorry, you look a bit like a friend of mine!

Good! The disguise has worked. I don't think she's recognised me!

Sponge man

All sorts of things may come in handy for making rod puppets, so keep a collection of bits and pieces. Garden canes and lengths of dowel from hardware shops make good rods.

To make a rod puppet like the one on this page you'll need a rod, an empty cheese box for the head, a small cardboard tube (cut in half) for the arms, some coloured paper, and, of course, a sponge! Paint the box and the tube before you stick your puppet together with strong glue.

Hats on!

Cut a circle of paper about 14cm across. Then cut a wedge out. Make a cone and tape it in place. Thread a length of elastic – long enough to fit round the cheese box – either side of the cone.

Cut some funny shaped hands from paper. Cut slits and slot them on to the ends of the tube

Use a pair of scissors to make a slit in the sponge and push the rod in

ARMS AND LEGS

So far the puppets we've used have not been able to move about much. But the rod puppets we've made here are a bit different!

Paint all the pieces before you put them together. Don't tie the hands and arms too tightly or they will not be able to move! Allow a little slack. Now try your puppet out! By twisting the rod in your hand you'll be able to make the puppet swing its arms. Try this slowly, and then very quickly.

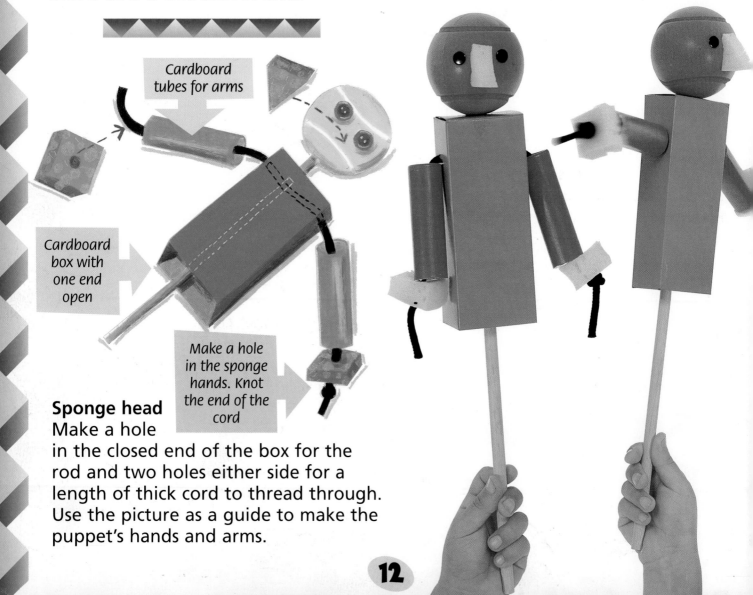

Cardboard tubes for arms

Cardboard box with one end open

Make a hole in the sponge hands. Knot the end of the cord

Sponge head
Make a hole in the closed end of the box for the rod and two holes either side for a length of thick cord to thread through. Use the picture as a guide to make the puppet's hands and arms.

TIPS

★ Practise moving your puppets around in front of a mirror. This will give you an idea of what the audience will see!

★ Make your puppets different sizes. They don't all have to be small!

Hey! Watch me move!

Use one rod to move the arm and the other to move the puppet

Shake hands!

Some rod puppets are made with two rods. The second rod operates one of the arms. This gives you more control over what your puppet can do.

Make the rods long enough so your hands will not show when you are performing

Draw a shape on card. Cut off one of the arms and use it as a pattern to make a slightly longer one. Attach the moving arm to the body with a split pin. Thread a length of string through the arm and knot it. Tie the other end to one of the rods. Glue the second rod to the back of the puppet.

STAGE STRUCK!

Now you are probably ready to try your puppets out on a stage! It's time to think about backgrounds, sound effects, and all the things that will help bring your puppets alive!

When you are making your theatre, bear in mind the size of your puppets!

From the bottom

All the puppets we've looked at so far are worked from below the stage and held above the puppeteer. This means you'll need a stage which hides your body and is big enough for you to move around in comfortably.

We made our stage from two cardboard boxes. The big one came from a shop that sells washing machines and fridges. Cut a panel in one of the sides of the big box so you can get in and out. Cut another panel in the top. With the small box you'll need to cut three panels – one for the front so the audience can see, one on the bottom for the puppets, and one on top for the backdrop.

Depending on the size of the box, you can either kneel or stand

Bring the play to life with a background scene

Decorate the boxes and stick them together with strong glue. Attach a piece of material at the side so the audience cannot see you! Paint a backdrop on a separate piece of paper – or make a paper collage. Glue the backdrop to a piece of dowel and balance it on top of the stage. Take your puppets inside and get some practise!

It's great being a puppet. You never get nervous in front of the audience!

If possible, make a small shelf inside your theatre to keep puppets that are not on stage

It's a bit of a squash with two of us in here but we'll manage!

TIPs

★ Large cardboard boxes are not easy to find! Ask local shopkeepers to save them for you.
★ Look out for our ideas later on for making 'instant' theatres.

Cut shapes from pieces of card, paint them and glue them to your theatre

Get a partner to help so you can see what the puppets look like from the front

SHADOWS

Shadow puppets are among the oldest puppets in the world. You'll need a special stage to show your puppets and a light source which you can find out about on the next page.

Make your puppets move with the help of a split pin and an extra rod

The plot comes first

As with all puppetry, it's important that you get your ideas, plot and characters sorted out first. Then the puppet making will be easy!

He looks a bit fierce, better steer clear!

Shadow puppets are most effective if they are black on the front

Through a screen

Shadow puppets are different from the other puppets we've looked at because the audience sees them through a screen. The shadows that appear on the front of the screen look quite mysterious. The puppets are operated close to the back of the screen, so it is best to attach the rods to the back of them at right angles.

Hold the rods fairly close to the puppet so you have control over it

Cut them out

Draw the outline shapes of your puppets on card and cut them out. It can look quite effective if you cut out small shapes from the main pieces.

If you are making a moving puppet, make sure you allow enough overlap on the separate pieces.

Practise in front of a mirror so you can see what your puppet is doing!

TIPS

★ Use thick card for your puppets so that they stand up to the wear and tear of performing.
★ Make your rods more secure by sticking a drawing pin through from the right side.

Make them work

For unjointed puppets, glue one rod to the back near the middle. For jointed puppets, make a hole through both pieces of card and push a split pin through. Glue one rod to the main puppet part and the other to the part that moves.

17

LIGHT UP!

As soon as you've made your shadow puppets and worked out the plot, you will need a theatre and a source of light to put on a show!

Frame and screen

Choose a solid cardboard box – not too deep – that will stand on its side without wobbling! This will be your shadow theatre.

Decorate

the outside of the box with paint, coloured paper and glitter for a sparkly effect. Prop your theatre on a table and shine a torch on the back of the screen.

Cut the bottom out of the box, leaving a frame round the outside. Lay a sheet of strong tracing paper over the frame and tape it all the way round.

Using daylight

A torch is fine for a small table-top screen, but if your screen is larger you may need to rig up a lamp to give enough light. The stronger the light source the clearer the shadows will be. Avoid using more than one light source because this will make your shadows appear blurred.

If you are putting your show on during the day you'll probably find that ordinary daylight will give you enough light. Bright sunlight is best! Whatever the source of light, your puppets must be operated between it and the screen.

Keep the rest of your puppets out of the way so they don't make a shadow on the screen. But not too far away!

Hey Max! Do you think you could teach me that dance!

PULL A STRING

String puppets are probably the most popular of all puppets. Unlike other puppets they are operated from above. Some puppets have lots of strings but it's best to start with a simple one!

Cheesy bird!
Both the chirpy bird puppets here were made from circular cheese boxes – a large one for the body and a small one for the head.

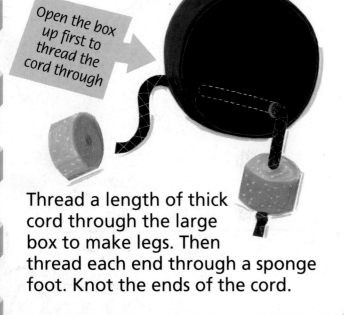

Open the box up first to thread the cord through

Thread a length of thick cord through the large box to make legs. Then thread each end through a sponge foot. Knot the ends of the cord.

Make a beak by cutting a semicircular section from a cheese box. This is tricky so you may need some help! Glue the beak onto the smaller box and then glue the whole of the bird's head onto its body.

Paint the pieces before you put them together

Crossbar and strings
String puppets are operated by moving strings attached to various parts of the puppet. The strings are tied to a crossbar and the puppeteer can make the puppet move by controlling the crossbar. You will see how this is done as soon as you have a go! Make the crossbar from two lengths of balsa wood. Wind string round the point where the pieces of wood cross to keep them in place.

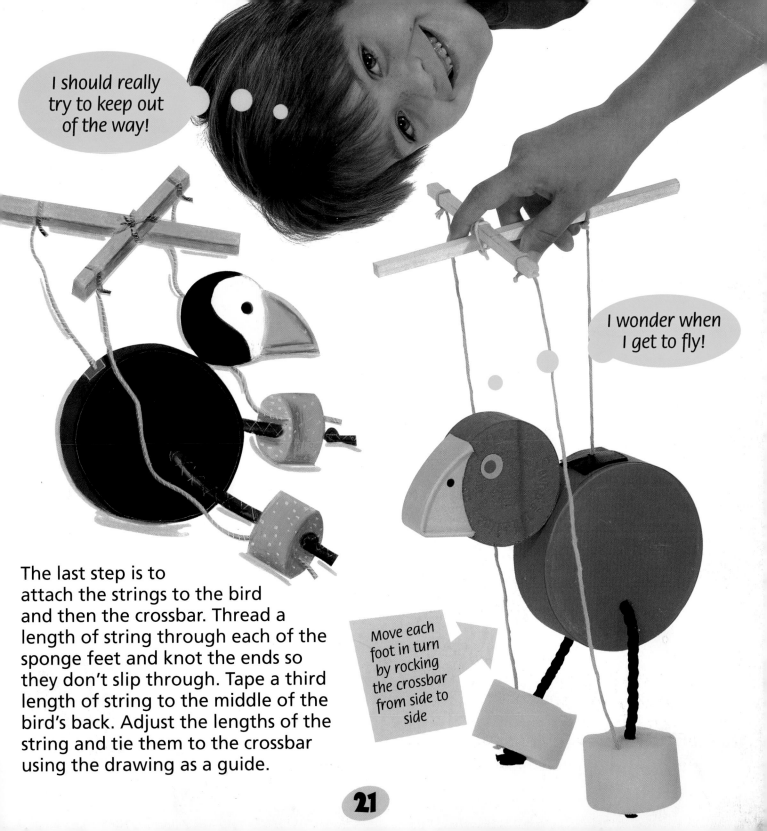

The last step is to attach the strings to the bird and then the crossbar. Thread a length of string through each of the sponge feet and knot the ends so they don't slip through. Tape a third length of string to the middle of the bird's back. Adjust the lengths of the string and tie them to the crossbar using the drawing as a guide.

ON ALL FOURS!

Now you know how string puppets work, try making one with four legs and a head that moves around!

Leave the boxes open until you have added the strings!

Spotty cow

Gather together some cardboard boxes to make your puppet's body, head and feet. The legs and neck can be made from thick shoelaces or cord.

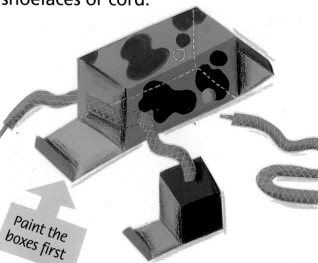

Paint the boxes first

Attach the head to the body with a length of cord. Add a tail, and you're nearly ready to add the strings! First you'll need to make a crossbar from three pieces of wood, tied together. Wind the string round and round where the pieces of wood join.

Make holes in the sides of the large box to thread the cord through. Thread the ends of the cord through each of the small boxes. Knot the ends to stop them slipping through!

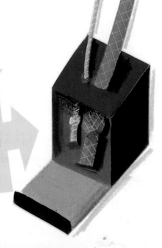

Ask a grown-up to help you make the holes

Adding the strings

Thread and knot lengths of string through each of the feet, alongside the cord legs. You'll also need a string in the middle of the head and the middle of the body. Adjust the lengths and use the photograph as a guide to tie the strings to the crossbar.

Off we go!

Now you can have some fun! Hold the long piece of the crossbar and by rocking it gently from side to side try to make the spotty cow lift each of its legs in turn. You can make him lie down, sit on his back legs and nod his head! What else can you do?

STRING SHOW

When you and your string puppets are ready to put on a show, you will need a different sort of stage because the puppets are operated from above!

▼▼▼▼▼▼▼▼▼

Setting the scene
There are all sorts of different ways to make stages for string puppets. We've chosen something very simple!

I've got the strangest feeling that I'm being followed!

Start with the background. Paint a scene on a large sheet of card or paper, or make a collage using shapes cut from coloured paper. If you use paper, glue it to a sheet of card afterwards to make it firm.

Make sure your backdrop will stand up on its own, leaving you free to operate your puppets. Cut two large right angle triangles from thick card. Score along one of the edges and fold back a flap. Use the flaps to tape the triangles to the back of the backdrop.

Sometimes you'll need to change backdrops between scenes. Make the new backdrops from paper and then you can simply attach them to your original board with large bulldog clips. This should only take seconds!

Extra props

You may want to add a few extras to your stage set to make it look more interesting. Here's an easy way to make a tree. Cut two 'tree' shapes from card. On one of them cut a slit from the top to the middle. On the other cut a slit from the bottom to the middle. Slot them together and stand the tree up.

I can't believe I haven't been spotted yet!

For a large backdrop, use more than two triangles

You can make all sorts of things using the slit and slot method

IT'S BIG!

Here's a chance to turn yourself into a giant puppet! and put on a really BIG show!

I could do with someone pulling my strings!

Don't bend your arms or legs!

Robo tricks

Try to find some corrugated card used for packing. It has ridges and bends easily. If not use thin card. Ask a friend to measure you. Cut out card tubes to fit round your head, body, arms and legs. Cut out shapes in the head piece for your eyes and mouth and cut two arm holes in the body. Paint the pieces and tape them together.

Put on the legs first, then the body, arms next and finally the head!

Ask a friend to help you put your outfit on

Behind you!

Here's another idea for a giant puppet. Tape together several sheets of newspaper. Lie down on the paper and ask a friend to draw round you. This will give you a pattern to cut your puppet pieces from.

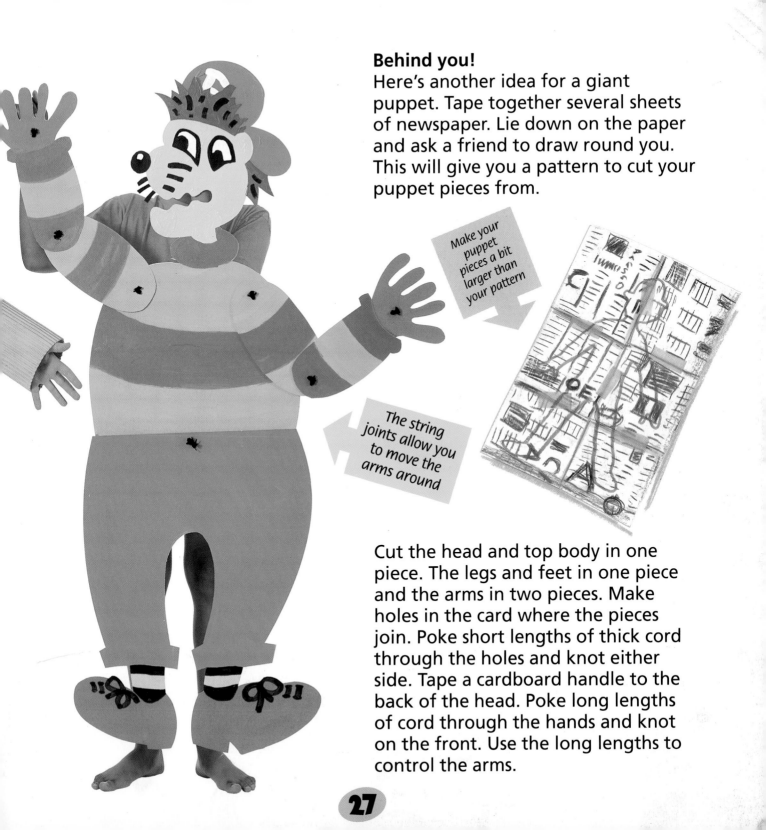

Make your puppet pieces a bit larger than your pattern

The string joints allow you to move the arms around

Cut the head and top body in one piece. The legs and feet in one piece and the arms in two pieces. Make holes in the card where the pieces join. Poke short lengths of thick cord through the holes and knot either side. Tape a cardboard handle to the back of the head. Poke long lengths of cord through the hands and knot on the front. Use the long lengths to control the arms.

GETTING READY

Here are a few hints and tips that may help when you come to put on a show for your friends and family.

Posters and invitations

Make sure as many people as possible know about the show well in advance. Make posters giving the time of the performance, date and name of the show. They should be as bright and colourful as possible. Send out invitations to your friends with the same information.

Don't be afraid to use all sorts of different puppets in your show

A helping hand

People will probably be only too happy to help with the performance. Make sure everyone has a special job and knows when it needs to be done! You may need help with puppet making, setting up the theatre or handing round drinks on the big day. Don't be afraid to ask!

Write it down

Because you'll have so much to remember on the day of your puppet show, it's a good idea to write lists of things to do. Give copies to the friends who are helping you.

There's just enough time for a final run through – costumes, music, sound effects...

Make sure your puppets are in perfect working order before the show

I'm sure everything will seem a lot better when I get my head together

Instant stage

Not only is this an easy stage to set up, it will work with all kinds of puppets. Crouch behind the curtain for rod and glove puppets. Or, stand behind to operate string puppets in front of the curtain.

SHOWTIME

The big day has arrived and the show must go on! Make sure everyone has a seat where they can see the stage and hear the puppets speaking.

> Ladies and gentlemen, welcome to the puppet show of the century!

> I hope she remembers my lines!

If you're using string puppets, hang them up before you use them so the strings don't get in a tangle

DON'T WORRY IF YOU FORGET YOUR WORDS! MAKE SOMETHING UP THAT WILL SOUND CONVINCING!

★

DON'T CHOOSE PLAYS WITH TOO MANY WORDS. ON THE WHOLE, PUPPETS ARE BETTER AT DOING THINGS RATHER THAN TALKING

★

REMEMBER THAT PUPPETS CAN DO COMPLETELY UNREALISTIC THINGS THAT PEOPLE CAN'T

Quick change

If you are including different sorts of puppets in your show, use a stage that will adapt easily. The audience will be grateful for a pause between acts and it will give you the chance to change props and scenery and make sure that you have the right puppets ready. Announce each different act and let the audience settle down before you start. Most important of all, take a big bow at the end of the show!

INDEX

backdrop 14, 15, 24, 25
background 14, 24
balsa wood 20
cord 12, 20, 22, 23, 27
cotton balls 8
crossbar 20, 21, 22, 23
dowel 11, 15
face flannel 8, 9
finger puppet 4, 6, 7
giant puppet 26, 27
glove puppet 8, 9, 29
invitations 28
mirror 17
mop 4, 10
pattern 9, 27
plot 16, 18
posters 28
props 4, 25, 31

rod 16, 17
rod puppet 10, 11, 12, 13, 29
scenery 4, 31
screen 16, 19
shadow puppet 4, 16, 17, 18, 19
shadow theatre 18, 19
shoelaces 22
sock puppet 8, 9
split pin 13, 17
sponge 11, 20
stage 4, 14, 15, 29, 31
stick puppet 10, 11
string 13, 20, 21, 22, 23
string puppet 4, 20, 21, 22, 23, 24, 25, 29, 30
torch 18, 19

You were great, but it's back in the box now till the next time!